"The gospel of Jesus is not like leaflets dropped from an airplane but rather a seed that takes root in people's lives, growing to bear fruit. If you are intimidated by evangelism, this book will help you find the freedom to let the gospel grow in the power of the Spirit, not in your own power."

— JERRY WHITE, PhD; major general,
U.S. Air Force, retired

ADVANCING THE GOSPEL

COLOSSIANS

"All over the world this gospel
is bearing fruit and growing."
— Colossians 1:6

MIKE TRENEER

NAVPRESS

Discipleship Inside Out®

NAVPRESS

Discipleship Inside Out®

NavPress is the publishing ministry of The Navigators, an international Christian organization and leader in personal spiritual development. NavPress is committed to helping people grow spiritually and enjoy lives of meaning and hope through personal and group resources that are biblically rooted, culturally relevant, and highly practical.

For a free catalog go to www.NavPress.com
or call 1.800.366.7788 in the United States or 1.800.839.4769 in Canada.

ISBN-13: 978-1-61747-157-5

Cover design by Arvid Wallen

Some of the anecdotal illustrations in this book are true to life and are included with the permission of the persons involved. All other illustrations are composites of real situations, and any resemblance to people living or dead is coincidental.

All Scripture quotations in this publication are taken from the *Holy Bible, New International Version*® (NIV®). Copyright © 1973, 1978, 1984 by Biblica, Inc.™ Used by permission of Zondervan. All rights reserved worldwide. WWW.ZONDERVAN.COM. The "NIV" and "New International Version" are trademarks registered in the United States Patent and Trademark Offices by Biblica, Inc.™

Library of Congress Cataloging-in-Publication Data
Treneer, Mike.
    Advancing the Gospel : how the Gospel bears fruit and grows / Mike Treneer.
        p. cm.
    ISBN 978-1-61747-157-5
1. Bible. N.T. Colossians—Commentaries.   I. Title.
    BS2715.53.T74 2011
    227'.7077—dc22   2011007860

Printed in the United States of America

2 3 4 5 6 7 8 9 10 / 17 16 15 14 13 12

NOTE FROM THE PUBLISHER

The book you hold in your hands has deeply influenced generations in the movement of discipleship to Jesus. The best books are timeless, and most often they cross cultural barriers. NavPress has placed this book in our NavEssentials series because it has stood the test of time and has shown the power to touch a new generation of disciples in many settings around the world.

Jesus said, "Every teacher of the law who has been instructed about the kingdom of heaven is like the owner of a house who brings out of his storeroom new treasures as well as old" (Matthew 13:52). At NavPress, we are conscious of both the old and the new, and we treasure both. We live in a world of profound change in publishing, and NavPress is at the forefront of keeping up with the new media. But we are also looking to our heritage to never forget where we have come from and to pass along those timeless Navigator messages that have proven to change lives.

The ministry of The Navigators began in the 1930s through the call of God to Dawson Trotman. Trotman's vision was to teach others, one to one, the biblical principles of discipleship he found beneficial in his own life. He began to teach high school students and local Sunday school classes. In 1933, he and his friends extended their work to reach out to sailors in the U.S. Navy. From there Trotman met and established a partnership with the then up-and-coming evangelist Billy Graham.

One of the men Trotman chose to lead the work with Billy Graham was Lorne Sanny. Sanny went on to become Trotman's successor and served The Navigators for thirty years as its president. The books in the NavEssentials series are what Lorne Sanny used to call "life-borne" messages. These are messages that grow out of a life steeped in the Scriptures and lived out in passionate love and obedience to God. They are tested in real life and have a practical authenticity that prompts genuine transformation. We call these NavEssentials "Voices of The Navigators—Past, Present, and Future."

Over the years, I personally have been touched by the messages in the NavEssentials series. Each one is part of the fabric of my own discipleship. I'm convinced that you, too, will find in them an abundance of godly stimulation and transformative guidance for your own walk with God.

DR. MICHAEL D. MILLER
president, NavPress
chief business officer, The Navigators

CONTENTS

CHAPTER 1

THE POWER OF THE GOSPEL SEED

Colossians 1:1-14

Colossians 1:1-14

¹Paul, an apostle of Christ Jesus by the will of God, and Timothy our brother,

²To the holy and faithful brothers in Christ at Colosse: Grace and peace to you from God our Father.

³We always thank God, the Father of our Lord Jesus Christ, when we pray for you, ⁴because we have heard of your faith in Christ Jesus and of the love you have for all the saints—⁵the faith and love that spring from the hope that is stored up for you in heaven and that you have already heard about in

the word of truth, the gospel [6]that has come to you. All over the world this gospel is bearing fruit and growing, just as it has been doing among you since the day you heard it and understood God's grace in all its truth. [7]You learned it from Epaphras, our dear fellow servant, who is a faithful minister of Christ on our behalf, [8]and who also told us of your love in the Spirit.

[9]For this reason, since the day we heard about you, we have not stopped praying for you and asking God to fill you with the knowledge of his will through all spiritual wisdom and understanding. [10]And we pray this in order that you may live a life worthy of the Lord and may please him in every way: bearing fruit in every good work, growing in the knowledge of God, [11]being strengthened with all power according to his glorious might so that you may have great endurance and patience, and joyfully [12]giving thanks to the Father, who has qualified you to share in the inheritance of the saints in the kingdom of light. [13]For he has rescued us from the dominion of darkness and brought us into the kingdom of the Son he loves, [14]in whom we have redemption, the forgiveness of sins.

The letter Paul wrote to the Colossians gives us an insight into how the gospel takes root and grows. As we read this letter we can ask ourselves how the gospel spread through the Roman Empire in the first century—and from that we can learn how the gospel spreads in our day, in the contexts in which God has placed us.

In the first hundred years of the Christian adventure, the gospel spread rapidly throughout the Roman Empire. The book of Acts shows us the panoramic view of the spread of the gospel as Paul, the other apostles, and the early believers traveled from place to place. But the New Testament letters, and especially this letter to the Colossians, open a window on what was happening in this one market town: Colosse, in the Roman province of Asia, about eighty miles inland from Ephesus, where Paul spent three years of his ministry. This letter to the Colossians shows how the gospel invaded the life of one small community and how it impacted the people there.

We learn from this picture how the gospel spreads, grows, and takes root in our lives, and in the lives of our friends and of many communities around the world today.

We start in Colossians 1:1-14.

The Seed of the Gospel

As Paul describes the way the gospel came to Colosse, he uses an agricultural illustration: "All over the world this gospel is bearing fruit and growing, just as it has been doing among you since the day you heard it and understood God's grace in all its truth" (verse 6). The picture reminds us of Jesus' parable of the sower. Jesus talked about the spread of the gospel—the spread of the kingdom of God—in agricultural terms. He said the kingdom was like a man going out and scattering seed on the ground. The seed takes root, germinates, and grows in different kinds of soil.

Paul has this idea in mind as he writes about the growth of the gospel in Colosse. He says the gospel is like a seed, and this gospel seed was sown by someone named Epaphras: "You learned it from Epaphras, our dear fellow servant, who is a faithful minister of Christ on our behalf" (verse 7). Epaphras, we learn later in the letter, was a Colossian, for Paul writes of him, "Epaphras, who is one of you and a servant of Christ Jesus" (4:12). This young man carried the gospel back home to Colosse and saw it take root and grow among his friends, family members, and contacts.

We don't know where Epaphras met Paul or first heard the gospel. But it seems likely that it was during the time Paul was ministering in Ephesus. Luke tells us in Acts 19:9-10 that Paul "had discussions daily in the lecture hall of Tyrannus. This went on for two years, so that all the Jews and Greeks who lived in the province of Asia heard the word of the Lord." Clearly all the province of Asia did not flock to hear Paul speak in the hall of Tyrannus, for Paul quite clearly says to the Colossians that he had never met them personally. But people in towns scattered through the province of Asia, including Colosse, Hierapolis, Laodicea, Smyrna, Pergamum, Thyatira, Sardis, and Philadelphia, heard the gospel because people like Epaphras carried it from Ephesus back to their home communities.

So the first lesson we learn about the spread of the gospel is that *the gospel spreads through people*. It is carried by ordinary people who embrace it and take it to their friends. Then we see that *the gospel spreads and grows like seed*. The power of the gospel is not atom-bomb power. It's not destructive power. It's seed power. Just as seeds need to fall into the ground and germinate, so Paul describes the germinating process of the seed of the gospel among the Colossians.

Look at verse 6 again: "All over the world this gospel is bearing fruit and growing, just as it has been doing among you since the day you heard it and understood God's grace and all its truth." How does the gospel germinate in a life? What is it that brings the gospel's power alive in a person? Paul says that it's hearing it and understanding it.

The Fruit of the Gospel

It's thrilling to think that this gospel is still bearing fruit and growing all over the world, as it was then. Today, as you read this, people are hearing and understanding the gospel for the very first time. This is particularly thrilling when we recognize the fruit of the gospel, as Paul describes it here among the Colossians.

Look at how he describes it in verses 4-6: "Because we have heard of your faith in Christ Jesus and of the love you have for all the saints—the faith and love that spring from the hope that is stored up for you in heaven and that you have already heard about in the word of truth, the gospel that has come to you."

What is the fruit of the gospel? It's the fruit of faith, hope, and love. This is the same fruit that I've experienced in my life, that you've experienced in your life, and that people all over the world are experiencing. Of course we see many other fruits as we read through the Scriptures. But the main characteristics of the gospel in a life or in a community are faith, hope, and love. Try to imagine what a society is like without faith, without hope, without love. Then think how a society or community, a life, a family is transformed when those fruits come—that's the blessing of the transforming power of the gospel.

Changes the Gospel Brings

This transformation the gospel brings is further explained in the following verses. Two types of change are described: invisible change and visible change. Paul describes visible change in verses 9-10: "We have not stopped . . . asking God to fill you with the knowledge of his will through all spiritual wisdom and understanding . . . that you may live a life worthy of the Lord and may please him in every way: bearing fruit in every good work, growing in the knowledge of God."

As we get to know one another, we can sense and see these outward changes: changes in our understanding, changes in our knowledge of God, changes in our behavior and in the way we live. But these changes are the result of invisible changes described in verses 12-14:

- "The Father . . . qualified you to share in the inheritance of the saints in the kingdom of light." Now, you can't look at someone walking down the street and discern this. You can't say "Look! There's someone who's been qualified to share in the inheritance of the saints in the kingdom of light!" It's an invisible change.
- "He has rescued us from the dominion of darkness." You can't say by outward observation, "There's Katie—she's been rescued from the dominion of darkness!" That rescue is an invisible change.
- "He . . . brought us into the kingdom of the Son he loves, in whom we have redemption, the forgiveness of sins." That's another invisible change.

It's important to realize that when the gospel invades a life, when the gospel is understood and believed and embraced, the first thing that happens is a set of absolutely incredible invisible changes—changes in our destiny and in our identity that result in changes in our outward life and behavior. That's the way the gospel changed the community in Colosse. That's the way the gospel changed Epaphras. That's the way the gospel changed me. That is the transforming power of the gospel.

So, how does the gospel spread and grow? First, it spreads through people. Ordinary people, like Epaphras. Then the gospel spreads and grows like seed that germinates and brings the fruit of faith, love, and hope into people's lives. The gospel produces change—dramatic, invisible changes in our destiny and our identity followed by visible change in our lives.

My own story illustrates the power of this change. As I walked across my university campus one day in 1966, I thought, *God, I don't like the person I'm becoming. Please help me.* Soon afterward I met a student involved in The Navigators who invited me to a meeting. To this day, I don't remember the message I heard that evening, but I vividly remember the student sitting next to me who asked if I was a Christian. "Yes, I've always been a Christian. My dad's a pastor," I answered.

His response surprised me: "Well, God doesn't have grandchildren. You can't become a child of God by being the son of a child of God." Then he opened the Bible and explained the gospel to me. That guy sitting next to me did for me what Epaphras did for his friends and family in Colosse. God used him to plant the gospel seed in my life that evening.

On that night when I understood and embraced the gospel for the first time, immense invisible changes took place in my life. God forgave my sins and redeemed me, and I was given eternal life in Christ. In Christ I received the gift of the Holy Spirit, I became an heir of the promises and was caught up in God's mighty purposes for our world. I'm still unpacking and understanding those changes today. Every day I discover new things that I received that first night when I understood and believed the gospel. There was an immediate change; there was a change in my identity; there was a change in my destiny. By God's grace, those invisible changes go on producing visible changes, changes that can be seen and experienced by my friends and family and those I come into contact with day by day.

As we get further into Colossians, we'll see that this ongoing change, which is manifested in our lives as the fruit of the gospel, becomes evident in all sorts of ways, in our life purpose, in our understanding of our relationship with God, in our character, and in our relationships.

Questions for Reflection and Discussion

1. How did the gospel come to you?
2. How did it take root in your life?

3. What fruit has it borne, what changes has it produced, both visible and invisible?
4. What could you do to become an "Epaphras" to your family, friends, and community?

CHAPTER 2

HOW THE GOSPEL TAKES ROOT

Colossians 1:15-29

Colossians 1:15-29

[15][The Son] is the image of the invisible God, the firstborn over all creation. [16]For by him all things were created: things in heaven and on earth, visible and invisible, whether thrones or powers or rulers or authorities; all things were created by him and for him. [17]He is before all things, and in him all things hold together. [18]And he is the head of the body, the church; he is the beginning and the firstborn from among the dead, so that in everything he might have the supremacy. [19]For God was pleased to have all his fullness dwell in him, [20]and

through him to reconcile to himself all things, whether things on earth or things in heaven, by making peace through his blood, shed on the cross.

[21]Once you were alienated from God and were enemies in your minds because of your evil behavior. [22]But now he has reconciled you by Christ's physical body through death to present you holy in his sight, without blemish and free from accusation—[23]if you continue in your faith, established and firm, not moved from the hope held out in the gospel. This is the gospel that you heard and that has been proclaimed to every creature under heaven, and of which I, Paul, have become a servant.

[24]Now I rejoice in what was suffered for you, and I fill up in my flesh what is still lacking in regard to Christ's afflictions, for the sake of his body, which is the church. [25]I have become its servant by the commission God gave me to present to you the word of God in its fullness—[26]the mystery that has been kept hidden for ages and generations, but is now disclosed to the saints. [27]To them God has chosen to make known among the Gentiles the glorious riches of this mystery, which is Christ in you, the hope of glory.

[28]We proclaim him, admonishing and teaching everyone with all wisdom, so that we may present everyone perfect in Christ. [29]To this end I labor, struggling with all his energy, which so powerfully works in me.

In the previous chapter, we considered how the gospel grows and spreads and saw the excitement of the gospel impacting the community of Colosse through Epaphras.

Now, as we read on in Paul's letter to this community, Paul turns our attention to Jesus, who is at the heart of the gospel. We see that the gospel (literally, the "good news") is the good news about Jesus. It's the wonderful message announcing the kingdom of Jesus. It's the announcement of His great rescue operation. It's the astounding, almost unbelievable, message that the Creator of the universe, the person who made everything and upholds everything, revealed Himself in the man Jesus. That's astoundingly good news!

Verses 15-20 tell us that in Jesus we have redemption, the forgiveness of sins. Jesus is the image of the invisible God, the firstborn over all creation. By Jesus, all things were created: things in heaven or on earth, visible and invisible, whether thrones or power or rulers or authorities. All things were created by Jesus and for Jesus. Jesus is before all things, and in Jesus all things hold together. Jesus is the head of the body, the church. Jesus is the beginning and the firstborn from among the dead, so that in everything Jesus might have the supremacy. For God was pleased to have all His fullness dwell in Jesus and through Jesus to reconcile to Himself all things, whether things on earth or things in heaven, by making peace through His blood, shed on the cross.

So, Jesus is the center of the gospel. There are some amazing things said about Jesus here that give substance to the good news.

The Good News About Jesus

The first great thing Paul says about Jesus is that He "is the image of the invisible God" (verse 15). Jesus is God in human form. If you want to know what God is like, you look at Jesus. When we read the Gospels and see the beauty, power, majesty, love, and compassion of Jesus' life, we begin to realize that this is what God is like. That view completely transforms our lives. I have seen over and over again during our years of ministry that young people without hope, with nothing to live for, would begin to grasp the idea that the Creator of the universe, the One who controls all things, is revealed in Jesus and that He loves them and is reaching out to touch their lives with His compassion and love. This realization begins to bring amazing hope, joy, confidence, and faith.

But somehow I think our familiarity with the Gospels and their stories about Jesus keeps us from grasping that amazing revelation of God. We need to go back and refresh ourselves and think about it again. That's what Paul is inviting us to do in these incredible words about Jesus.

Jesus is also the firstborn over all creation. By Jesus

all things were created. I can't live, I can't breathe, I can't look at the colors and people around me without experiencing God, because He made it all. Everywhere we go, the whole of creation shouts at us about who Jesus is. When we make the link that Paul makes here, that this man who is the center of the gospel is the Creator, we begin to touch at the heart of this good news that is so life transforming.

The great tragedy of our world then is that it is rebelling. The glorious God who made all this beauty, who expresses Himself in the gentleness, love, humility, and servant heart of Jesus, is resisted, spurned, and mocked. What is the result? Our world is in chaos. It is full of sadness and sickness and misery and grief and pain and sorrow. But the gospel tells us that this God didn't just walk away from the beauty of His creation. He didn't walk away from the potential of our lives or the lives of every young person growing up in every slum of this world. Rather, He came personally as the rescuer, the Redeemer.

Look at how Paul describes this in verses 19-20: "For God was pleased [an incredible word, especially when you think of what it cost] to have all his fullness dwell in [Jesus], and through [Jesus] to reconcile to himself all things, whether things on earth or things in heaven, by making peace through his blood, shed on the cross."

So, the gospel is the good news—not only that Jesus is God, amazing though that is. And not only that He is the Creator and upholder of all things. And not only that He is the one to whom everything should submit. But Jesus has reconciled us to God through His death on the cross.

At the heart of the gospel is the picture of Jesus— the Creator of the universe, Lord of everything, knowing that everything is in His power—being nailed to a cross and praying, "Father, forgive them, for they do not know what they are doing" (Luke 23:34). That's the gospel. That's the good news about Jesus that, when sown into the lives of people, brings such an incredible transformation in this sin-sick, sad, suffering, miserable world where there is so much pain and unhappiness because of our rebellion against God.

The gospel brings about the fruit of faith and hope and love: "Once you were alienated from God and were enemies in your minds because of your evil behavior. But now he has reconciled you," Paul tells a little group of believers in that market town. They are now part of the solution and not part of the problem. The apostle continues, "He has reconciled you by Christ's physical body through death to present you holy in his sight, without blemish and free from accusation—if you continue in your faith, established and firm, not moved from the hope held out in the gospel. This is the gospel that you heard and that has been proclaimed to every creature under heaven, and of which I, Paul, have become a servant" (verses 21-23).

Embracing the Good News

Paul then describes how this message transformed his life and turned him from being an enemy of the gospel into an agent of the gospel—one who poured out his life to see other people experience the faith and hope and love the gospel brings. That's what the gospel does for all of us. When we embrace it, when we begin to understand it, the gospel turns us into its servants. We become joyful messengers carrying this seed into every situation into which God puts us.

"I rejoice in what was suffered for you," Paul says in verse 24, because the gospel involves suffering. It cost Jesus, and it costs those who carry it because of the hostility of this world and the spiritual opposition to this message. Then Paul makes this amazing statement: "I fill up in my flesh what is still lacking in regard to Christ's afflictions, for the sake of his body, which is the church" (verse 24). What on earth does that mean? I don't think it means that anything needs to be added to what Jesus did on the cross, but that those of us who have embraced the gospel need to be willing to embrace whatever suffering is needed in order for the gospel to reach people.

Paul then writes about "the commission God gave me to present to you the word of God in its fullness." He describes the gospel as "the mystery that has been kept hidden for ages and generations, but is now disclosed to the saints. To them God has chosen to make known among the Gentiles the glorious riches of this mystery, which is Christ" (verses 25-27). This is the Christ we've been talking about who is God, the Creator, the Lord of all, our Savior. The one who is "Christ in you, the hope of glory. We proclaim him, admonishing and teaching everyone with all wisdom, so that we may present everyone perfect in Christ. To this end I labor, struggling with all his energy, which so powerfully works in me" (verses 27-29). Once we really understand and believe, we become carriers of the gospel and, like Paul, our commitment to labor in the gospel leads us to do all we can to see that people fully understand and really experience the gospel's transforming power.

When we set this statement in the context of the first small group of believers in Colosse, and we ask why the gospel of Christ was spreading so powerfully, this chapter lets us see a picture of it. We see the way the gospel comes, the way it transforms, and the way it turns those who receive it into messengers and carriers of the gospel. The more we embrace and think about this good news of Jesus and all that Scripture tells us about Him, the more we long to be able to live that out and articulate it in ways that are meaningful to our friends. Even though it may involve suffering and struggle and difficulty, the gospel spurs those of us who receive it to become carriers of it to our friends, just as Paul was.

Questions for Reflection and Discussion

1. What aspects of the good news about Jesus mean the most to you?
2. Jesus is the invisible God made visible. What are you learning about what God is like by looking at Jesus?
3. As with the apostle Paul, the gospel turns us from being God's enemies into servants of the gospel. What does it mean for you to be a servant of the gospel in your situation?
4. What suffering might be involved in your being a faithful servant of the gospel?

CHAPTER 3

WHAT IMPEDES THE GOSPEL'S GROWTH

Colossians 2:1-23

Colossians 2:1-23

¹I want you to know how much I am struggling for you and for those at Laodicea, and for all who have not met me personally. ²My purpose is that they may be encouraged in heart and united in love, so that they may have the full riches of complete understanding, in order that they may know the mystery of God, namely, Christ, ³in whom are hidden all the treasures of wisdom and knowledge. ⁴I tell you this so that no one may deceive you by fine-sounding arguments. ⁵For though I am absent from you in body, I am present with you in spirit

and delight to see how orderly you are and how firm your faith in Christ is.

[6]So then, just as you received Christ Jesus as Lord, continue to live in him, [7]rooted and built up in him, strengthened in the faith as you were taught, and overflowing with thankfulness.

[8]See to it that no one takes you captive through hollow and deceptive philosophy, which depends on human tradition and the basic principles of this world rather than on Christ.

[9]For in Christ all the fullness of the Deity lives in bodily form, [10]and you have been given fullness in Christ, who is the head over every power and authority. [11]In him you were also circumcised, in the putting off of the sinful nature, not with a circumcision done by the hands of men but with the circumcision done by Christ, [12]having been buried with him in baptism and raised with him through your faith in the power of God, who raised him from the dead.

[13]When you were dead in your sins and in the uncircumcision of your sinful nature, God made you alive with Christ. He forgave us all our sins, [14]having canceled the written code, with its regulations, that was against us and that stood opposed to us; he took it away, nailing it to the cross. [15]And having disarmed the powers and authorities, he made a public spectacle of them, triumphing over them by the cross.

[16]Therefore do not let anyone judge you by what you eat or drink, or with regard to a religious

festival, a New Moon celebration or a Sabbath day. [17]These are a shadow of the things that were to come; the reality, however, is found in Christ. [18]Do not let anyone who delights in false humility and the worship of angels disqualify you for the prize. Such a person goes into great detail about what he has seen, and his unspiritual mind puffs him up with idle notions. [19]He has lost connection with the Head, from whom the whole body, supported and held together by its ligaments and sinews, grows as God causes it to grow.

[20]Since you died with Christ to the basic principles of this world, why, as though you still belonged to it, do you submit to its rules: [21]"Do not handle! Do not taste! Do not touch!"? [22]These are all destined to perish with use, because they are based on human commands and teachings. [23]Such regulations indeed have an appearance of wisdom, with their self-imposed worship, their false humility and their harsh treatment of the body, but they lack any value in restraining sensual indulgence.

We have seen in Colossians 1 how the gospel spreads and how it centers on the person of Jesus. As Paul shared his own response to the gospel, we also saw how embracing the good news turns us into servants of the gospel.

Now, in Colossians 2, we move into a part of the book where Paul expresses his concerns for this small group of believers in Colosse. He addresses the things that threaten their faith and growing community. As he shares his struggle for them, we learn about things that threaten our lives spiritually and how to respond to those threats.

First, we should notice that Paul had never met the Colossians. Their faith was the fruit of the labor of Epaphras. They were Paul's spiritual grandchildren and great-grandchildren, and his deep concern and earnest prayer for them is evidence of Paul's generational vision for the multiplying impact of his ministry in the province of Asia. As we reflect on these verses we can learn not only about the dangers that threaten the fruit of the gospel in our own lives but also about the things that can hinder the generational impact of the gospel through our ministry to others.

Paul's concern for the Colossians centers on his desire for them to understand as fully and deeply as possible all there is to know and experience in the person of Christ and the good news about Him. His concern leads him to give them four warnings. I'd like to identify them and then see how he encourages the Colossians to respond to these dangers.

Threats to Our Spiritual Lives

Paul wants the Colossian believers to grasp all that they have in Christ and what can keep them from experiencing it.

Fine-sounding arguments. The first warning is in verse 4. He says, "I tell you this so that no one may deceive you by fine-sounding arguments." There is a danger for this new group of believers. If they don't go deep into understanding the message of Christ, they are going to be deceived by someone who comes along with great new ideas and they will be diverted or distracted from the message of the gospel.

Deceptive philosophy. In verse 8 Paul picks up the warning again and adds a new twist: "See to it that no one takes you captive through hollow and deceptive philosophy, which depends on human tradition and the basic principles of this world rather than on Christ."

In the Roman Empire of those days there was a real danger of an outburst of persecution and hostility. In fact, Paul wrote this letter while he was in prison. But he's not warning them here about the danger of a physical prison. Instead, he's warning them of a mental prison. It's possible to have prisons in our minds. In fact, I think we all have those prisons—beliefs that box us in, that stop us from living to the full potential of who God has made us to be. We just don't believe it's possible to be all that God wants us to be.

Paul is very concerned for these believers. They face a real danger of failing to live out to the fullest extent all God has for them simply because of wrong ideas.

Unjust judging. Paul warns of another danger in verse 16: "Do not let anyone judge you by what you eat or drink, or with regard to a religious festival, a New Moon celebration or a Sabbath day." This is revolutionary thinking. In human societies, people are usually kept in line by how others judge or perceive them. But the gospel introduces a whole new way of transformation—from the inside out, not by an enforced conformity to how other people think we should live.

Exaggerated spiritual claims. The last warning is in verses 18-19: "Do not let anyone who delights in false humility and the worship of angels disqualify you for the prize. Such a person goes into great detail about what he has seen, and his unspiritual mind puffs him up with idle notions. He has lost connection with the Head." This is another danger from well-meaning, zealous, religious enthusiasts who feel they've got the latest thing—be it visions or angels.

Response to These Dangers

Notice Paul's solution to these dangers that can sidetrack us and block us from maturity in Christ.

Focus on Jesus. In verses 4-5 he says, "I tell you this so that no one may deceive you by fine-sounding arguments. For though I am absent from you in body, I am present with you in spirit and delight to see how orderly you are and how firm your faith in Christ is." He takes them from the danger back to Christ.

In verse 8 he says, "See to it that no one takes you captive through hollow and deceptive philosophy, which depends on human tradition and the basic principles of this world *rather than on Christ*" (emphasis added).

How do we deal with the prisons in our minds? How do we guard our minds from wrong ideas? From the world around us? From the way we've been brought up? We must go to Christ. You remember that Jesus said to the Jews who were believing in Him, "If you hold to my teaching, you are really my disciples. Then you will know the truth, and the truth will set you free" (John 8:31-32). It is as we come to Jesus and give attention to what He said that the light of the truth penetrates the darkness of our minds and reveals the wrong ideas—the prisons—that are there. We believe His Word, and it breaks down the lies.

It's very good sometimes to sit with a group of friends and ask, "What are the basic principles of this world? What are the big ideas that shape the society in which we live? Are they true?" One of those big ideas, for example, is that you can't be happy without acquiring more material possessions or increasing your standard of living. Though the idea is not true, it drives and controls the lives of millions of people.

Or you can turn the questions to our "human traditions." What are the ideas that you were brought up believing? Many of them are good, but some may not be quite so good. What are the ideas you're sowing in the minds of young people? Are they really according to Christ?

These are important things to think about. Unless we identify these big ideas that dominate our lives and test them carefully with the teaching of Jesus, we will live in a prison, boxed in, unable to experience life as God means for us to experience it.

The answer to all these dangers is to come back to Jesus. At the heart of this chapter—in fact, at the heart of this book—comes this exhortation: "So then, just as you received Christ Jesus as Lord, continue to live in him, rooted and built up in him, strengthened in the faith as you were taught, and overflowing with thankfulness" (verses 6-7).

Rooted and built up. Receiving Christ is a great beginning, but we have to build on that beginning. We have to continue in Christ. Paul is exhorting these Colossians, "As you have begun, so continue, rooted and built up in Christ."

He uses two metaphors here. One is the illustration we saw earlier, of a rooted plant. Plants grow by sending down roots. That's the picture Paul uses to talk about how we grow in Christ. By faith and by secret prayer and by meditating and reflecting on God's Word, we can draw on the resources of God that energize, enrich, beautify, and cause us to grow into our full potential in Christ. Paul is giving us a beautiful picture of how we grow to maturity in Christ.

His second picture is of being "built up" in Christ. The Greek word Paul uses here refers to building a house. Unlike the growth of a plant, which is a natural process, being built up is a human process. Of course, human beings help plants grow as well by nurturing them and watering them. But buildings are a particularly human thing. Our growth in Christ involves human effort. So this double metaphor of being "rooted and built up" reminds us that growth in Christ is a partnership in which we work with Him, building into the lives of those in whom spiritual growth is taking place by the inner working of God. As Paul writes to the Philippians, "Continue to work out your salvation . . . for it is God who works in you" (Philippians 2:12-13).

Strengthened in the faith. We also respond to these dangers by being "strengthened in the faith as you were taught" (verse 7). The word *taught* brings to mind the concept of learning in a school or a class. Growing in Christ involves learning things. If I had studied for my math or engineering exams in college as most people "study the Scriptures" in their Christian lives, I wouldn't have done very well. I put in a lot of effort to learn things that were important to me. In the same way, we're not going to grow in Christ as we should unless we are committed learners, and unless we are committed to being taught and to continuing in the things that we are taught.

Overflowing with thankfulness. Paul then uses a beautiful picture of "overflowing with thankfulness" like a glass being filled to overflowing (verse 7). It's another way our lives grow in Christ, as if we become glasses into which God pours His love until it overflows with thankfulness to those around us.

So, how do we guard against the danger of being sidetracked, of being stunted Christians and not growing to our full potential? We focus on Christ.

All That We Have in Christ

After preaching in Nairobi one day, I received a startling phone call. A woman who wouldn't give her name said she heard me share the gospel but believed life wasn't worth living. She was planning to end her own life. I could tell there were "prisons" in her mind that only God's Word could break through. She didn't want to meet face-to-face so I asked her to ponder Psalm 139, Ephesians 1, and the last half of Romans 8 and to promise not to do anything until she had phoned back to tell me what she learned from them.

Days later she called back and said the verses had helped. I asked her to memorize the most helpful ones, and from time to time over the coming weeks she called to talk about them. The truth of Christ began to break down the prisons in her mind.

Three years later, a radiant young woman came up to me after I spoke at the same church. She introduced herself as the woman who had been calling. When I saw her, the transforming power of the gospel was abundantly clear, the power of God's truth that breaks through our mental prisons and reveals Christ.

In verses 9-15, Paul mentions eight things about who Jesus is and what He has done for us. Paul is pushing the Colossians to understand that they have far more in Christ than they have grasped. There is more to experience; there is more to be enjoyed; there is more to know; there is more to understand. As we unpack the treasure chest of all Christ is, we discover more and more of His fullness and all that He has done for us. The big challenge for all of us is that we become committed students of the Scriptures, of Jesus, and of His teaching so we're always discovering more of what He's done for us, more of who He is, and more and more of how that works out in our lives.

Questions for Reflection and Discussion

1. What are the most dangerous threats to your continued growth in Christ? Which "prisons" are you aware of in your life?
2. Can you identify the biggest lies influencing the world around you and how these lies impact you?
3. What are the major factors helping you continue to grow in Christ?
4. What steps could you take to understand more fully and deeply all that Jesus is and all that you have in Him?

CHAPTER 4

TAKE TIME TO TEND THE GARDEN

Colossians 3:1–4:1

Colossians 3:1–4:1

[1]Since, then, you have been raised with Christ, set your hearts on things above, where Christ is seated at the right hand of God. [2]Set your minds on things above, not on earthly things. [3]For you died, and your life is now hidden with Christ in God. [4]When Christ, who is your life, appears, then you also will appear with him in glory.

[5]Put to death, therefore, whatever belongs to your earthly nature: sexual immorality, impurity, lust, evil desires and greed, which is idolatry. [6]Because of these, the wrath of God is coming.

[7]You used to walk in these ways, in the life you once lived. [8]But now you must rid yourselves of all such things as these: anger, rage, malice, slander, and filthy language from your lips. [9]Do not lie to each other, since you have taken off your old self with its practices [10]and have put on the new self, which is being renewed in knowledge in the image of its Creator. [11]Here there is no Greek or Jew, circumcised or uncircumcised, barbarian, Scythian, slave or free, but Christ is all, and is in all.

[12]Therefore, as God's chosen people, holy and dearly loved, clothe yourselves with compassion, kindness, humility, gentleness and patience. [13]Bear with each other and forgive whatever grievances you may have against one another. Forgive as the Lord forgave you. [14]And over all these virtues put on love, which binds them all together in perfect unity.

[15]Let the peace of Christ rule in your hearts, since as members of one body you were called to peace. And be thankful. [16]Let the word of Christ dwell in you richly as you teach and admonish one another with all wisdom, and as you sing psalms, hymns and spiritual songs with gratitude in your hearts to God. [17]And whatever you do, whether in word or deed, do it all in the name of the Lord Jesus, giving thanks to God the Father through him.

[18]Wives, submit to your husbands, as is fitting in the Lord.

[19]Husbands, love your wives and do not be harsh with them.

[20]Children, obey your parents in everything, for this pleases the Lord.

[21]Fathers, do not embitter your children, or they will become discouraged.

[22]Slaves, obey your earthly masters in everything; and do it, not only when their eye is on you and to win their favor, but with sincerity of heart and reverence for the Lord. [23]Whatever you do, work at it with all your heart, as working for the Lord, not for men, [24]since you know that you will receive an inheritance from the Lord as a reward. It is the Lord Christ you are serving. [25]Anyone who does wrong will be repaid for his wrong, and there is no favoritism.

[4:1]Masters, provide your slaves with what is right and fair, because you know that you also have a Master in heaven.

We're following Paul as he unpacks the gospel for these first believers in Colosse and helps them think through its implications for the way they live.

In Colossians 3, Paul's letter gets very practical and personal about the fruit that God expects in our lives and relationships. Notice that Paul starts by focusing on how the gospel changes our lives and character. Then he moves into the way that the gospel changes our relationships.

How the Gospel Changes Our Lives

In the first ten verses of chapter 3 Paul addresses two responses to the gospel: actions of faith and of repentance. I like to think of this passage as spiritual gardening. If you let your garden go natural, all the good plants you wanted to grow get overwhelmed by the weeds that seem to come whether you want them or not. Our lives are like that in this fallen world. So as we receive the seed of the gospel into our lives, we've got to become spiritual gardeners. By faith we nurture the fruit of the gospel, and by repentance we deal with the weeds that keep springing up.

A response of faith. Notice that as Paul describes our ongoing faith response to the gospel, he gives a two-part action we need to take.

Verse 1 says, "Set your hearts on things above, where Christ is seated at the right hand of God." We associate our hearts with our affections, our emotions. But then he also says in verse 2, "Set your minds on things above, not on earthly things." I don't know what helps you with that faith response of focusing your mind and your heart. One of the most consistently helpful things for me has been to take time each day when I specifically focus my mind and my heart.

The gospel teaches us the importance of being centered on Christ. That's what Paul is talking about here. Take time each day to set your mind and your heart on things above. It's a faith response to the gospel and Paul gives his readers "faith convictions" to strengthen their resolve for their faith response. He writes, "You have been raised with Christ . . . Christ is seated at the right hand of God. . . . You died, and your life is now hidden with Christ in God. When Christ, who is your life, appears, then you also will appear with him in glory" (verses 1,3-4).

A response of repentance. There is also a repentance response to the gospel: "Put to death, therefore, whatever belongs to your earthly nature" (verse 5). This is the weeding part of our spiritual gardening. Paul buttresses the action of repentance with what I call "repentance convictions." Just as we saw in our faith response that there are things we believe and ways we act because of those beliefs, the same is true with repentance. "You used to walk in these ways, in the life you once lived," Paul says. "But now you must rid yourselves of all such things as these" (verses 7-8). He then mentions some weeds: "anger, rage, malice, slander, and filthy language from your lips. Do not lie to each other, since you have taken off your old self with its practices and have put on the new self" (verses 8-10).

The idea that we have "put on the new self" is a new conviction that buttresses our repentance resolve. We're putting on the new self "which is being renewed in knowledge in the image of its Creator" (verse 10). Now that is a glorious thing to believe. The battle I'm fighting with the weeds in my spiritual garden is something God is working in me as I work on it.

That's where Paul starts with the change in our lives, with this spiritual gardening idea. But then he quickly carries that forward into the way this impacts our relationships.

How the Gospel Changes Our Relationships

Here again Paul starts with underlying convictions then talks about character qualities and actions that build relationships.

Belief systems. The gospel is always taking us back to what we believe, because ultimately we live out of what we believe. That's where we were in Colossians 2, you'll remember, with the prisons in our minds. So as we want to see our relationships affected by the gospel, we can't start by trying to deal with our relationships. We start by going under the surface of our lives to look at our root systems.

Paul makes two amazing statements about our belief systems. First, he says, "Here there is no Greek or Jew, circumcised or uncircumcised, barbarian, Scythian, slave or free, but Christ is all, and is in all" (verse 11). This means we respond to one another as believers as we would respond to Christ. What we believe transforms the way we respond to one another: You look at me and I look at you, and we see Christ in each other. This is a gospel conviction that produces the fruit of love and Christlike relationships among us.

Paul goes on to say, "Therefore, as God's chosen people, holy and dearly loved, clothe yourselves with compassion, kindness, humility, gentleness and patience" (verse 12). Again, he is addressing who we are in Christ. He is saying, "You are God's chosen person, holy and dearly loved." Believing we are chosen, holy, and dearly loved addresses deep needs in us. All of us have a need for love. I think it is true that all people go into a new group asking, "Do you love me?" We're sort of like big "love vacuum cleaners" trying to see if there is any love there we can draw on. Emotional immaturity is not being able to get beyond that deep need for love. So, we go into every relationship as "getters."

But in Christ, God meets that deep need for love by assuring us of His love. He allows us to go into relationships in any context not asking primarily, "Do you love me?" but knowing that we're chosen and holy and dearly loved by God Himself. That frees us to go into relationships not as a drain but as a spring. We enter a group as someone asking, "How can I show you God's love for you?"

Of course, that disposition overflows, as Paul describes here, "With compassion, kindness, humility, gentleness and patience. Bear[ing] with each other and forgiv[ing] whatever grievances you may have against one another. Forgiv[ing] as the Lord forgave you. And over all these virtues put[ting] on love, which binds them all together in perfect unity" (verses 12-14).

Character qualities. I like to examine in two groups the qualities that flow from our deep recognition of

Christ in others and our deep sense of being loved. First are those character qualities that express the love of Christ to others: compassion, kindness, and gentleness. Compassion is something that starts inside of us. It's me sitting here thinking not *How am I feeling?* but *How are you feeling?* I wonder what's going on in your life. I wonder how I can show the love of Christ to you in a meaningful way. Compassion expresses itself in gentleness and kindness.

The second group of character qualities are also fruits of the gospel. They describe my responses to other people's actions, attitudes, and words. They are qualities such as humility, patience, forbearance, and forgiveness. The fact is, we live in a fallen world. However hard we try to express love and kindness, we get it wrong sometimes. Weeds are sometimes expressing themselves in our relationships because of the spiritual gardening we haven't been doing, and we end up hurting people—intentionally or unintentionally. That happens with all of us; even when we try to be loving and considerate we can end up hurting people around us, and often we are not trying. And that is true of everyone else too. Even the people who love me most can hurt me deeply, not to mention all the people who don't love me! So we need not only qualities that reach out to express love but also qualities that allow us to respond to the sometimes hurtful behavior of others in a way that is Christ-honoring and Christlike.

When we look back at those early Colossian believers and imagine relationships like this happening, we begin to see why the gospel spread so powerfully. The gospel spread through the Roman Empire not primarily because the first believers were great preachers but because they were people of compassion, kindness, patience, and forgiveness. The early non-Christian writers who bear witness to the growth of the gospel most often describe the kindness and compassion of Christians. They describe the way believers reached out to the broken and the sick and the suffering people around them. These Christians created communities of love and grace that were powerfully attractive to those around them and led to the gospel being not just heard but experienced and embraced by those who were watching and listening. The fruit of the gospel has seed in it!

Actions. Paul goes on to describe not only the convictions that shape our relationships and the character qualities that build our relationships but also the actions that build our relationships of trust. Let's pick that up in verses 16-17: "Let the word of Christ dwell in you richly as you teach and admonish one another with all wisdom, and as you sing psalms, hymns and spiritual songs with gratitude in your hearts to God. And whatever you do, whether in word or deed, do it all in the name of the Lord Jesus, giving thanks to God the Father through him."

What did the early Christians do together to build their sense of community and their relationships in Christ? We could summarize it as *Word, worship,* and *work.*

Word. The early Christians, as Paul exhorts them to do, allowed the Word of Christ—the teaching of Christ—to be central to what they did: "Let the word of Christ dwell in you richly as you teach and admonish one another with all wisdom" (verse 16).

If we want to build the kinds of relationships we're talking about here, we put the Word of God at the center of what we do. We meet together to study and reflect on the words of Christ.

Worship. Worshipping together, whether in large or small groups, changes the dynamic of our relationships with one another. When we turn our attention from the horizontal dynamics of our interactions with each other to the vertical dynamic of focusing on God together, it has an amazing way of changing our relationships. Hearing one another express love and thankfulness to God changes how we see and think about one another. And worshipping together invites the Spirit of God to live in us in a rich and filling way.

Work. Finally, Paul says, "Whatever you do, whether in word or deed, do it all in the name of the Lord Jesus, giving thanks to God the Father through him" (verse 17). We shouldn't be afraid of doing things together as Christians. We're not going to build our sense of community simply by sitting in a circle and studying the Bible together. Building this kind of community is going to mean doing things together that express our faith and love for the Lord. It means thinking of ways we can get out and serve Him in our communities and express His love in practical ways to people in word and deed.

The Changes Expressed in Everyday Life

Now Paul takes us into the different spheres of our lives. In the next verses he describes how these changes the gospel brings affect not only our working environments but also our family environments.

I want especially to notice one important principle that was absolutely revolutionary in the first-century world to which Paul was writing: "Wives, submit to your husbands, as is fitting in the Lord. Husbands, love your wives and do not be harsh with them" (verses 18-19). These commands and the ones that follow express a *reciprocal responsibility*: "Children, obey your parents in everything, for this pleases the Lord. Fathers, do not embitter your children, or they will become discouraged. Slaves, obey your earthly masters in everything; and do it, not only when their eye is on you and to win their favor, but with sincerity of heart and reverence for the Lord. Whatever you do, work at it with all your heart, as working for the Lord, not for men. . . . Masters, provide your slaves with what is right and fair, because you know that you also have a Master in heaven" (3:20-23; 4:1).

We see a reciprocal responsibility throughout these verses. The recognition of reciprocal responsibility in relationships was absolutely revolutionary and transforming. In the Roman world might was right. Husbands, fathers, and masters had absolute rights over their wives, their children, and their slaves. But Paul teaches that receiving God's love and forgiveness brings an obligation to learn to relate in all our relationships in mutually supportive ways.

North American society has been influenced deeply by this Christian concept, but it has swung over to the other extreme. From one end of the spectrum, where "might is right," we've swung over to the other extreme where "rights is right." But here the concept is one of mutual responsibility, as Paul summarizes in Ephesians 5:21 where he says, "Submit *to one another* out of reverence for Christ" (emphasis added).

May the Lord help us live this out in every context into which He has put us, in every relationship into which He has put us. This is where most people experience the gospel. You know, a friend of mine used to say, "The translation of the gospel that most people read is the translation into daily living."

I saw that vividly one day at the sprawling Elmina Castle on the coast of Ghana. The castle's dark dungeons and iron shackles are reminders of its past, when the British used it as a slave trading post, and countless Africans were forced into slavery in Europe and the Americas. Today, the castle is a popular destination for men and women in search of their roots.

As I toured this castle with a dear Ghanaian Christian friend, I was struck with a realization. My Ghanaian friend had every reason to hate me for what my ancestors had done. But instead, I experienced love and grace from him. Why? Because we were one in Christ. We were experiencing the power of the gospel, which transforms relationships anywhere and everywhere when the gospel is believed and embraced.

Questions for Reflection and Discussion

1. What do you find most helpful in setting your heart and mind on things above?
2. As you tend the garden of your soul, life, and character, which weeds do you find to be the most persistent?
3. How do these weeds affect your relationships?
4. What practical steps can you take to nurture the fruit of the gospel in your life and relationships?

CHAPTER 5

PARTNERING TO SOW GOSPEL SEEDS

Colossians 4:2-18

Colossians 4:2-18

²Devote yourselves to prayer, being watchful and thankful. ³And pray for us, too, that God may open a door for our message, so that we may proclaim the mystery of Christ, for which I am in chains. ⁴Pray that I may proclaim it clearly, as I should. ⁵Be wise in the way you act toward outsiders; make the most of every opportunity. ⁶Let your conversation be always full of grace, seasoned with salt, so that you may know how to answer everyone.

⁷Tychicus will tell you all the news about me. He is a dear brother, a faithful minister and fellow

servant in the Lord. [8]I am sending him to you for the express purpose that you may know about our circumstances and that he may encourage your hearts. [9]He is coming with Onesimus, our faithful and dear brother, who is one of you. They will tell you everything that is happening here.

[10]My fellow prisoner Aristarchus sends you his greetings, as does Mark, the cousin of Barnabas. (You have received instructions about him; if he comes to you, welcome him.) [11]Jesus, who is called Justus, also sends greetings. These are the only Jews among my fellow workers for the kingdom of God, and they have proved a comfort to me. [12]Epaphras, who is one of you and a servant of Christ Jesus, sends greetings. He is always wrestling in prayer for you, that you may stand firm in all the will of God, mature and fully assured. [13]I vouch for him that he is working hard for you and for those at Laodicea and Hierapolis. [14]Our dear friend Luke, the doctor, and Demas send greetings. [15]Give my greetings to the brothers at Laodicea, and to Nympha and the church in her house.

[16]After this letter has been read to you, see that it is also read in the church of the Laodiceans and that you in turn read the letter from Laodicea.

[17]Tell Archippus: "See to it that you complete the work you have received in the Lord."

[18]I, Paul, write this greeting in my own hand. Remember my chains. Grace be with you.

As we've followed Paul's letter to the Colossians, we have been prompted to think about how the gospel came to them; the change it produced in their lives; their dynamic, growing relationship with Christ; and the influence of that growth on their relationships with others.

We are now moving into the last part of the letter in which Paul invites the believers at Colosse to partner with him in the advance of the gospel. He closes by describing the contribution of twelve people to the gospel's advance. This illustrates the way God uses all types of people in all sorts of ways to become His partners in this incredible process of transformation.

Partnering Through Prayer

First, Paul invites the believers in Colosse to be partners with him in prayer: "Devote yourselves to prayer, being watchful and thankful. And pray for us, too, that God may open a door for our message" (verses 2-3). One of the thrilling things about the power of prayer is that it allows us to contribute to the lives of people all over the world without any restrictions of distance or accessibility. As I go back to our home church in the United Kingdom, one thing that constantly moves me is that people will come up and tell me, "Mike, we pray for your family every week" or "We pray for you daily." I wonder, how much of what happens in our lives happens because of these prayers? The Scriptures record many examples of the privilege of prayer in allowing us to contribute to the transforming power of the gospel in the lives of our friends.

Paul invites them to *devote* themselves to prayer. It's an interesting choice of words, isn't it? What does "devote yourself" conjure up to you? It doesn't sound like something you do halfheartedly, does it? It's something that becomes a major part of your life. Luke 5:16 records that Jesus Himself often withdrew to lonely places to pray.

Paul adds that he wants them to devote themselves to prayer, "being watchful and thankful" (verse 2). *Watchful* is also an interesting word to associate with prayer. Watchful for what? Things we should pray about? Ways in which God answers our prayers? I think probably at least those two things. We must also be thankful in our prayers. Prayer is the way by which we focus the power and the energy of God onto the lives of our friends and our loved ones.

Partnering Through Our Message

We can partner with others in Christian work as well, as Paul invites the Colossians to do here. He says, "And pray for us, too, that God may open a door for our message, so that we may proclaim the mystery of Christ, for which I am in chains. Pray that I may proclaim it clearly, as I should" (verses 3-4). I think it is very clear here that one of the ways in which we partner with God is through our message. We pray for God to open a door for us to *speak*.

It's not that we want to jump on people and dump the gospel on them. I think I did some of that as a young Christian. I would sense an opportunity with one of my friends and try to give him everything from Genesis to Revelation in one go. I would leave him reeling with spiritual indigestion or worse. Instead, we are to speak in a sensitive, loving way that is responsive to people's needs. As Paul goes on to say, "Be wise in the way you act toward outsiders; make the most of every opportunity. Let your conversation be always full of grace, seasoned with salt, so that you may know how to answer everyone" (verses 5-6).

When we answer the challenge of partnering with God in the advance of the gospel, we also want to be people who learn to explain the gospel clearly. When I think of the night I first really understood the gospel, I am so thankful to God that the young man I sat next to that evening was someone who learned to explain the gospel simply and clearly, from the Bible, in language I could understand. That's something we can all learn to do.

Now, we've got to remember that as we partner with God, we are partnering with *God*. It doesn't all depend on us. God has His people in positions of influence everywhere. He has you exactly where He wants you. If He wanted someone else in your network of friends and family, He would have put someone else there. He wants *you* there. He wants to express His love through you. He wants you to learn to pray for your friends and family. He wants you to learn to share your faith. But He wants to do it through the dynamics of who you are.

As You Are, Where You Are

I find it very beautiful that Paul ends this letter with a description of people who contributed to the advance of the gospel in Colosse.

Tychicus. "Tychicus will tell you all the news about me," Paul says. "He is a dear brother, a faithful minister and fellow servant in the Lord. I am sending him to you for the express purpose that you may know about our circumstances and that he may encourage your hearts" (verses 7-8). Tychicus was a person who was available to travel. Not everyone is. But Tychicus was the kind of person who could come into situations, whom Paul could ask to go and visit Christians in another place. A lot of my work has been like that— traveling into different situations and coming along-side and trying to encourage the people of God in that situation, bringing them news from elsewhere and taking news of them back. It's an important contribution, but it's not a primary contribution for everyone, though we may all have the opportunity to do this from time to time.

Onesimus. Tychicus was coming with Onesimus. He was a runaway slave returning to the household he had run away from—Philemon's household (the story is in the short letter of Philemon). Onesimus probably wished he could become a missionary. I'd guess it was hard to return and work as a slave in a household you'd run away from. But God had Onesimus exactly where He wanted him. We're still feeling the impact of Onesimus's faithfulness all these years later because he was prepared to be where God wanted him to be and to do what God wanted him to do.

Paul says that Onesimus is "our faithful and dear brother, who is one of you" (verse 9). If Tychicus was an "alongsider," coming into situations from the outside to encourage, Onesimus was an "insider"—someone called to be in the place where God sent him and live out his faith and witness there.

Aristarchus, Mark, and Barnabas. "My fellow prisoner Aristarchus sends you his greetings, as does Mark, the cousin of Barnabas. (You have received instructions about him; if he comes to you, welcome him)" (verse 10). It is fascinating to trace the stories of Mark, Barnabas, and Aristarchus throughout the rest of the New Testament and learn about them and from them. Mark was a writer who gave us the gospel of Mark, despite an early failure that disqualified him from being part of Paul's team for a while.

Barnabas's name means "son of encouragement." He was the one who stuck with Mark after his failure and got him back on track. He also encouraged Paul early on and drew him into the work at Antioch.

Aristarchus was from Thessalonica and helped Paul develop the ministry in Ephesus, where he had the distinction of being dragged into the arena by a mob. He came safely through the ordeal but later accompanied Paul to Rome and was in the shipwreck on the island of Malta. He certainly had some stories to tell of his missionary adventures when he got home to Thessalonica.

Jesus/Justus. "Jesus, who is called Justus, also sends greetings" (verse 11). We don't know anything else about this man. He's not mentioned anywhere else in the New Testament.

Epaphras. Now, we're back with Epaphras. He, you remember, is the one who first brought the gospel back to his own people there in Colosse. Listen to what Paul says about him: "Epaphras, who is one of you and a servant of Christ Jesus, sends greetings" (verse 12). Isn't that beautiful? It's not surprising that the gospel flowed through Epaphras's life, because the dynamic of being someone through whom the gospel moves is exactly captured in those two phrases: He's "one of you" and he's "a servant of Christ Jesus."

During the Beijing Olympics I was enthralled to watch the final of the women's 4 x 400 relay. It was certainly an exciting race as the American team overhauled the Russian team in the last few meters. But what I found most exciting was to see Allyson Felix lead her teammates in prayer at the end of the race. Who in the world has the power to call a prayer meeting in the middle of the Olympic arena in Beijing? Allyson Felix does! Why? Because she is a true insider, she has the respect of her teammates (she ran the fastest lap in the race), she is "one of them," but she is also "a servant of Christ Jesus."

Most people come to faith through a Christian friend. That was certainly the way it was with me. I came to faith through a friend I hung out with and played soccer with. But he was also a servant of Christ Jesus.

Listen to how Paul goes on to describe Epaphras: "He is always wrestling in prayer for you, that you may stand firm in all the will of God, mature and fully assured." Wouldn't you like to have a friend like that? How about being a friend like that? Paul says, "I vouch for him that he is working hard for you and for those at Laodicea and Hierapolis" (verses 12-13).

Luke, Demas, and Nympha. Then Paul talks about "our dear friend Luke, the doctor," who sent greetings along with Demas (verse 14). And Paul adds his own greetings: "Give my greetings to the brothers at Laodicea, and to Nympha and the church in her house" (verse 15). We don't know anything else about Nympha, but she opened her home so believers could meet and experience Christian fellowship and friendship together.

Archippus. And then there is this: "Tell Archippus: 'See to it that you complete the work you have received in the Lord'" (verse 17). We have no idea who Archippus was or what his work was. But I find that admonition very beautiful because each of us has a different work to do for the Lord. We're uniquely positioned to be agents of the gospel in our spheres and contexts exactly as God wants us to be. I think the Lord is saying to us, through Paul's exhortation to Archippus, "See to it that you fulfill your work in the Lord." Find out why God has you where He has you, and be there and do it with all your heart.

Paul. Paul concludes the letter by saying, "I, Paul, write this greeting in my own hand. Remember my chains. Grace be with you" (verse 18).

Twelve different people, all mentioned by name, all serving God in different ways, contributing to the progress of the gospel two thousand years ago in what we now call Turkey. Through their lives, they saw the gospel spread and bring the faith and hope and love of Christ in transforming ways.

We're caught up in the same thing. God has us engaged where we are, in our generation, in this place, as partners with Him—through our prayers, through our lives, through our message, through our friendships.

Questions for Reflection and Discussion

1. Practically, what does it mean for you to devote yourself to prayer, being watchful and thankful?
2. With whom are you currently partnering to advance the gospel? How would you describe

their special contribution to the partnership?
And yours?

3. Paul describes Epaphras as "one of you and a servant of Christ Jesus" (verse 12). Identify the lost people around you who would consider you to be "one of them." What does it mean to be a servant of Christ among them?

4. Paul's message to Archippus was "See to it that you complete the work you have received in the Lord" (verse 17). What would that look like for you?

ABOUT THE AUTHOR

MIKE TRENEER grew up in rural England. The son of a Church of England vicar, Mike found it hard as a teenager to relate to church and faith. He came to a personal relationship with Jesus through a Navigator ministry at Loughborough University of Technology. After graduation, Mike married Chris and they committed their lives to spreading the gospel. In the early 1970s, they led a student ministry in England before starting and developing a Navigator ministry in Nigeria. In 1981 and for the next seventeen years, Mike served as The Navigators' director for Africa before being named international vice president of the ministry. Since 2005, Mike has served as The Navigators' international president. Mike and Chris live in Colorado Springs, Colorado, and have three adult children who are active in ministry.

GLEN EYRIE

SUPPORT THE MINISTRY
OF THE NAVIGATORS

The Navigators' calling is to advance the gospel of Jesus and
His kingdom into the nations through spiritual generations
of laborers living and discipling among the lost.

Navigators have invested their lives in people for more than 75 years,
coming alongside them life on life to help them passionately know
Christ and to make Him known.

The U.S. Navigators' ministry touches lives in varied settings, including
college campuses, military bases, downtown offices, urban neighborhoods,
prisons, and youth camps.

Dedicated to helping people navigate spiritually, The Navigators aims
to make a permanent difference in the lives of people around the
world. The Navigators helps its communities of friends to follow Christ
passionately and equip them effectively to go out and do the same.

To learn more about donating to The Navigators' ministry,
go to **www.navigators.org/us/support**
or call toll-free at **1-866-568-7827**.

THE NAVIGATORS®